D0563816

LYNDON BAINES JOHNSON

From the time he was a boy in Texas, Lyndon Baines Johnson worked long and hard. First he was a schoolteacher, then a Congressman, then a Senator, and at last President of the United States. This is an easy-to-read story about L.B.J., about his early years, and about his marriage to Lady Bird. It is a story that tells about a great man.

Other SEE AND READ
Beginning to Read Biographies

GEORGE WASHINGTON
ABRAHAM LINCOLN
CHRISTOPHER COLUMBUS
POCAHONTAS
DANIEL BOONE
NATHAN HALE
JOHN FITZGERALD KENNEDY

To my Cub Scout grandson

David Scott Olds

who chose President Johnson as the subject

of his Hobby Book

A SEE AND READ
Beginning to Read Biography

LYNDON BAINES JOHNSON

by Helen D. Olds

illustrated by Paul Frame

G. P. Putnam's Sons New York

Library of Congress Catalog Card Number: 65-20714
MANUFACTURED IN THE UNITED STATES OF AMERICA Published simultaneously in the Dominion of Canada by Longmans Canada Limited, Toronto 07209

Third Impression

A boy called Lyn faced his three younger sisters, who were lined up before him. His brother, Sam, stood at his side. All of them were barefooted, and their faces were red from the sun.

They were standing by the barn of their farm in the hill country of Texas. Lyn looked past the barn to the fields. He could see the pony he rode to school every day. But now it was summertime and school was out.

"I need your help, kids," Lyn began. "Daddy's left me in charge of the farm while he's away. That's because I'm the oldest—nearly ten. And I've got to see to it that the work's done."

He looked down at his hands. They hurt from milking the cows. He had been up before breakfast to do the milking.

"I'll chop the wood," he went on. "And Sam can help me feed the pigs. But there are still the chickens to be fed."

Rebekah, the oldest sister, said, "I'll help."

"Me, too," added the two smaller sisters.

"All right, then. Get to work!" said Lyn.

The five of them hurried about, and the work was quickly done.

Lyn chopped a big pile of wood. Rebekah looked at it and smiled at her brother, Lyn. "Well, nobody can say you don't do your part of the work," she said.

Sam added, "You are a good boss, Lyn. I reckon you'll be a big ranch boss someday."

"Oh, no!" broke in Rebekah. "Remember what Granddaddy said when Lyn was born?" She tried to stand tall like her grandfather. She tried to make her voice sound deep and grown-up.

"Granddaddy said, 'A United States Senator was born today. His name is Lyndon Baines Johnson.' "

“Oh, you!” Lyn was tired of that story.

“I’ll give you a better story than that,” he told the others. “Maybe I’ll have time to read to you this afternoon.”

“Oh good!” they said. One sister added, “But I want a really true story. The kind *you* like, Lyn.”

All four of them wanted to be just like their big brother.

Not long after that, Lyn's family moved to Johnson City, Texas. The town had been named for the children's grandfather, the first Sam Johnson. Lyn's father and mother owned a newspaper there.

Lyn liked living in town. There were more things for him to learn than on the farm. After school he spent some of his time as a shoe-shine boy.

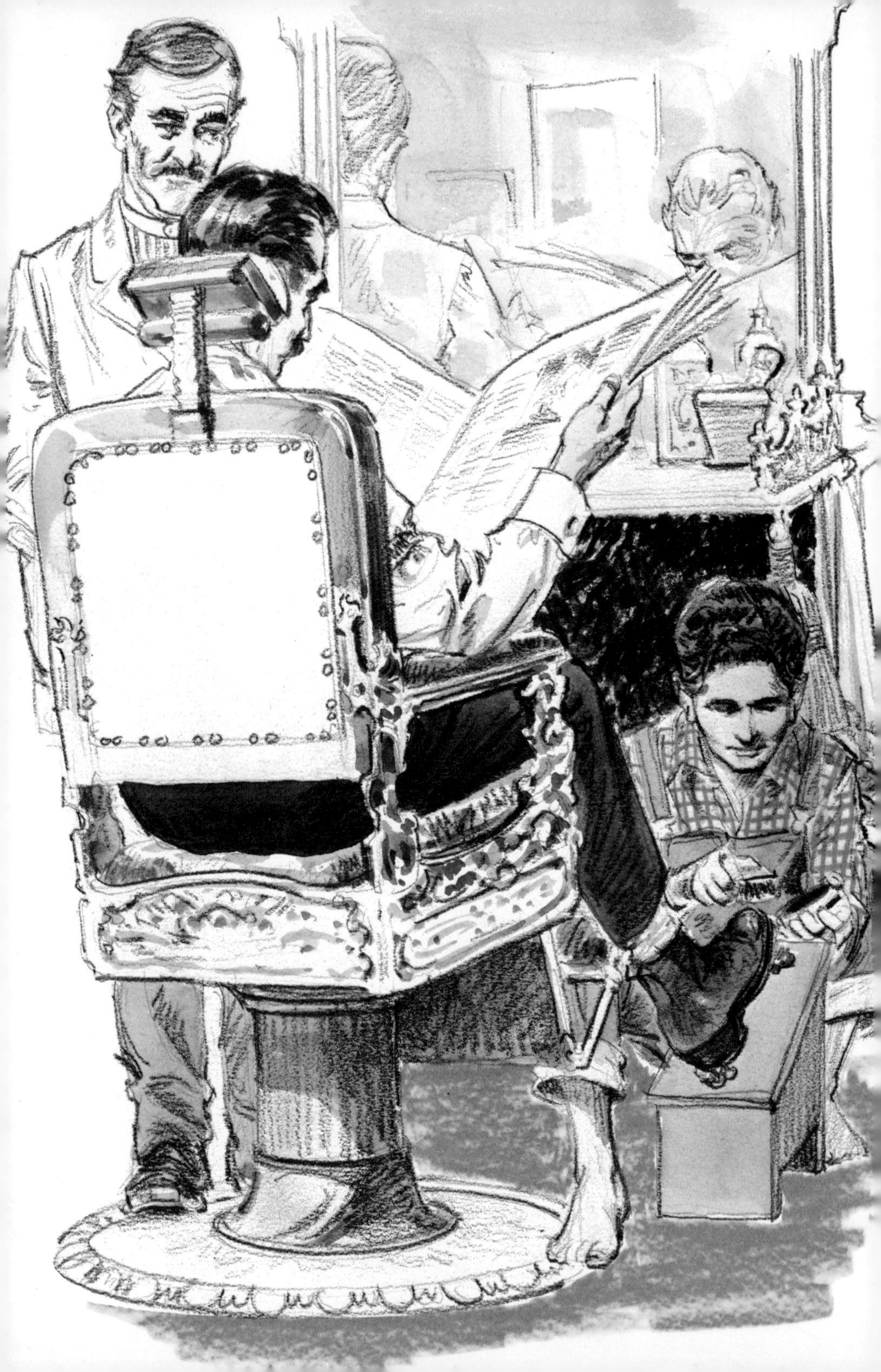

One day Lyn was in the barber shop shining a man's shoes. The man was to give a talk that evening. Lyn knew that his mother had written about it for the newspaper. A picture of the man would be in the paper too.

The man was saying, "Yes, it's a good thing to put an ad in the paper."

Lyn thought that over. He needed more business. If strangers came to town they would not know that Lyn shined shoes.

“I should put an ad in the paper,” he thought.

He finished the man’s shoes. Then he hurried to his mother at the newspaper plant. It was not far away.

"Have you gone to press yet?" he asked his mother.

"You know I haven't. Not until two o'clock." She looked up over the piles of yellow paper on her table. The big press was in the back room.

"I want to put an ad in today's newspaper," Lyn told her. "I'll pay for it, too."

Then he took a piece of paper and wrote on it:

If YOU WANT A GOOD SHINE
TRY LYN JOHNSON
AT THE BARBER SHOP

"I want it to go on page one," he said.

His mother said nothing. But she took the paper into the back room.

Lyn wondered all the afternoon, until the newspaper came out. Would his ad be on the front page?

It was! Lyn read it over and over, as he went back to the barber shop. He was standing there when a car drove up on the other side of the street.

A man was driving, and another man was sitting beside him. Lyn saw that the second man was his father. He had forgotten he was to come home this afternoon from a trip.

As Lyn watched, the car stopped, and his father bought a newspaper from a newsboy. He looked at the front page.

What would his father think about the ad? Lyn looked down at his bare feet.

He heard his father laugh. Then he heard him speak. "To think, I had to own a newspaper so my wife could tell the world that our son is a shoe-shine boy!" Lyn's father laughed again, but he sounded proud.

The years went by, and Lyn was ready for high school. He was tall and straight. In high school he did some public speaking and found he enjoyed it.

When he finished high school, he did not want to go to college. "I'm through with school," he said to his mother.

His mother looked sad. She and Lyn's father had both hoped he would go to college.

But Lyn just wanted to go away, to see new places. He and five of his friends went to California where they hoped to find work. When they arrived in California, they had no money left. And they could not find work.

So Lyn came home again. His mother was glad to see him. She told him, "Remember what Granddaddy said—that you would be a United States Senator? To be a Senator you should go to college."

Lyn thought a while. Then he said, "All right. I'll give college a try."

He went to a town near Austin, the capital of Texas. There he entered a state college, to learn to be a teacher.

Soon Lyn was the star speaker for the college. He worked to earn money. He washed floors and cleaned blackboards, trying out his speeches while he worked.

He finished college in 1930 and then taught public speaking at a high school in Houston.

He liked the school, but after one year, a Texas Congressman came to him with a question. He was going to Washington, D.C., the capital of the United States. Would Lyndon like to come along and work for him? Lyn did not have to be asked twice. He was ready to go.

"I like teaching," he said. "But you can help more people in politics."

By now Lyndon was tall and good-looking. All the girls liked him. Then one day when Lyndon was in Austin, he met Lady Bird Taylor.

She was a small girl with a nice smile. She and Lyndon looked at each other. Lyndon said, "I'm pleased to meet you, Ma'am." He liked her right away. "May I see you again tomorrow?" he asked. Lady Bird smiled a friendly "yes."

The next day, Lyndon found himself telling her all about himself and his family. He felt she was the girl for him.

They were married in the fall of that year. After a trip to Mexico, young Mr. and Mrs. Johnson went to Washington to live.

Then Lyndon learned that Lady Bird did not know how to cook!

She learned fast. Not only about cooking, but about politics, and how to give talks.

At this time, Lyndon Johnson was working hard for the young people of the United States. He helped them to find work.

He saw to it that the cities had parks and playgrounds for the children. He worked hard for the Negroes and Mexicans so that they would have better homes to live in.

His work was praised by Franklin Roosevelt, who was then President of the United States. Lyndon admired President Roosevelt very much and was glad that he, too, was in politics.

When he had been married three years, he was elected Congressman.

"Perhaps some day you'll be President," Lady Bird said to him.

Lyndon thought about that. The Presidency was the biggest job in the world, he knew. President Roosevelt was busy from morning to night.

A President was the head of the Army and Navy. He had to report each year to Congress on the state of the Union.

He had to tell Congress about laws that he felt were good. And he had to see that the laws were followed.

He had to meet newspaper people, be in parades, go to dinners, make speeches, and do a hundred other things.

"Well," said Lady Bird, "I'm sure you would make a good President."

Then in 1941, America entered World War II. Lyndon Johnson joined the Navy and was made a Lieutenant Commander. He was in the Navy until 1942, when Congressmen were called back.

Lyndon and Lady Bird had two children. The first one they named Lynda Bird, the second Lucy Baines.

"Some day, we may be sorry about the L.B.J.'s," Lady Bird said. "It will be hard for us to know which things belong to which L.B.J."

Soon Lyndon's friends were asking him to run for Senator from Texas. He had run for the Senate seven years before, but he had lost. Would he lose this time?

He went to Texas in a helicopter. Through a loudspeaker, he spoke to the men and women working in the fields. He told them he wanted to be their Senator, and that he would help them.

Lady Bird, Lyndon's mother, and his three sisters did their part, too. They telephoned everyone in the telephone book and asked them to get out and vote!

Lyndon Johnson won the election. "I'll be the best Senator these folks ever had," he said.

He worked hard and got many laws passed. They were laws that made our country better. They helped the people living in places where there was not enough rain to grow food.

They helped Texas to get more water for the farms and cities. They helped the farmers to get telephones. They helped the men who had been in our country's war.

Senator Johnson made his helpers work hard, but he himself worked even harder. It was just the way it had been when he was young. Then he had wanted his brother and sisters to do their part of the farm work. He did his part then, and he was doing his part now — and more!

The years went by. In 1960, John F. Kennedy was running for President. He picked Lyndon B. Johnson to run for Vice-President.

"Lyndon is a fine man," said John Kennedy. "He is the best man I know in American politics. He really cares about this country as I want a Vice-President to care."

He and Johnson were elected to the highest offices in the land.

Lady Bird knew that Lyndon Johnson would try to be the best Vice-President the country ever had. She went on trips with him. They went all over the world and they made friends everywhere.

The Vice-President would jump out of the car to shake hands with everyone.

He went into people's homes to visit with them. Some of these homes were only huts.

He made friends abroad, just as he had in Texas.

Three years passed. Then one day in November, Lyndon Johnson and Lady Bird went to a big city in Texas, with the President and Mrs. Kennedy.

There was a big parade. It started out as a happy day. President Kennedy and his wife were riding in an open car.

Suddenly a man shot at President Kennedy, from the high window of a building. The President was hit.

President Kennedy was hurried to the hospital, but he died soon after reaching it. People throughout the country and all over the world were very sad.

Almost at once, Lyndon Johnson, Mrs. Johnson and Mrs. Kennedy were rushed to a plane going back to Washington. As the plane flew north, Lyndon Johnson took the oath of office that made him thirty-sixth President of the United States.

A little later, Lyndon Johnson, the tall Texan, spoke to the people of this country.

All over the world folks were listening to their radios and watching their television sets. People leaned nearer to their sets, trying to hear every word.

Then the new President spoke. "This is a sad time for all people," he said. "I will do my best. That is all I can do. I ask your help, and God's."

And he did his best in the year that followed.

Soon it came time for the people to vote again for a President. Lyndon Johnson ran against Barry Goldwater.

Hubert Humphrey ran for Vice-President with Johnson, as Lyndon Johnson had run with John Kennedy four years before.

Lyndon Johnson and Hubert Humphrey won the election. Now Lyndon Johnson was President in his own right.

He had a ten-point plan. Some of the things he wanted to do were to help children learn better, to learn about space, to take care of older people, to fight against sickness, and to help other nations.

Everyone felt it was a good plan.

Everyone knew that Lyndon Johnson would work hard at being a good President.

Key Words

Army	Navy	Senate
capital	newspaper	Senator
college	oath	space
Congress	office	speech(es)
Congressman	parade(s)	telephone
elect(ed)	politics	television
law(s)	President	Union
Lieutenant Commander	press	Vice-President
nation(s)	public	vote
	radio	

The Author

HELEN D. OLDS attended college in her home town of Springfield, Ohio, and studied journalism for two years at the University of Texas. In addition to writing some twenty-five books for children and conducting writing courses at various colleges and universities, Mrs. Olds has raised a family that now includes five grandchildren. *Christopher Columbus* was her first SEE AND READ Biography. The author lives in Little Neck, Long Island.

The Artist

PAUL FRAME lives in New York City where he is active in many phases of educational work at Friends Seminary. He has illustrated biographies of Robert Frost, Horace Greeley and John Fitzgerald Kennedy, as well as *The Boy With One Shoe, Honestly, Katie John!,* and *Casey at Bat.* In addition to book illustrations, Mr. Frame also does advertising art.